easy star. 5

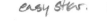

FAVORITE FOOTBALL TEAMS

OAKLAND RAIDERS

BY K. C. KELLEY

S

THE CHILD'S WORLD®

1980 Lookout Drive • Mankato, MN 56003-1705
800-599-READ • www.childsworld.com

ACKNOWLEDGMENTS

The Child's World®: Mary Berendes, Publishing Director
Shoreline Publishing Group, LLC: James Buckley, Jr., Production Director
The Design Lab: Kathleen Petelinsek, Design; Gregory Lindholm, Page Production

PHOTOS

Cover: Focus on Football
Interior: AP/Wide World: 4, 9, 10, 17, 18; Focus on Football: 7, 13, 21, 22, 23, 25, 27; Stockexpert: 14

LIBRARY OF CONGRESS
CATALOGING-IN-PUBLICATION DATA

Kelley, K. C.
  Oakland Raiders / by K.C. Kelley.
      p. cm.
  Includes bibliographical references and index.
  ISBN 978-1-60253-318-9 (library bound : alk. paper)
  1. Oakland Raiders (Football team)—Juvenile literature. I. Title.
  GV956.O24K45 2009
  796.332'640979466—dc22   2009009068

Printed in the United States of America
Mankato, Minnesota
December, 2009
PA02038

TABLE OF CONTENTS

Go, Raiders!

Pirates playing football? Not real pirates, of course! These football "buccaneers" are the Oakland Raiders. Their **logo** looks like a pirate's flag. Their team colors are silver and black. They play tough, hard football . . . just the kind pirates might play! The Raiders have had many great teams over the years. Their fans are almost as famous as the players! Let's find out more about this swashbuckling football team.

I scored, I scored! Javon Walker celebrates after scoring a touchdown for the Raiders in a 2008 game.

Who Are the Oakland Raiders?

The Oakland Raiders play in the National Football League (NFL). They are one of 32 teams in the NFL. The NFL includes the National Football Conference (NFC) and the American Football Conference (AFC). The Raiders play in the West Division of the AFC. The winner of the NFC plays the winner of the AFC in the **Super Bowl**. The Raiders have been the NFL champions three times!

Here are the Raiders at the line of scrimmage, ready to start their next play. This team is known for its tough offense! The Raiders' silver and black uniforms are among the NFL's most famous.

Where They Came From

The Raiders began in another league—the American Football League (AFL). The AFL was active from 1960 to 1969. The Raiders played in the AFL for all of that league's 10 seasons. They won the 1966 AFL Championship. They also played in the second Super Bowl. In 1971, the AFL and the NFL joined together. By 1977, the Raiders were the NFL champions! In 1982, the team moved to Los Angeles. They played there until 1995, when they moved back to Oakland.

Longtime Raiders owner Al Davis lifted the Super Bowl trophy in 1984 while his team cheered!

Who They Play

The Raiders play 16 games each season. There are three other teams in the AFC West. They are the Denver Broncos, the Kansas City Chiefs, and the San Diego Chargers. Every year, Oakland plays each of these teams twice. All four teams used to be in the AFL. They have been **rivals** for many years! The Raiders play other teams in the NFC and AFC, too.

Games between the Raiders and the Broncos are often tough battles. Neither team wants to lose to the other!

Where They Play

The Raiders play their home games at Oakland Coliseum. This stadium is right beside San Francisco Bay. It is also home to baseball's Oakland Athletics. Special seats roll onto the baseball field to change the Coliseum into a football stadium. When the Raiders played in Los Angeles, they played at the enormous L.A. Memorial Coliseum.

Here, the Raiders are playing a home game at the Oakland Coliseum. Thousands of fans are watching them!

13

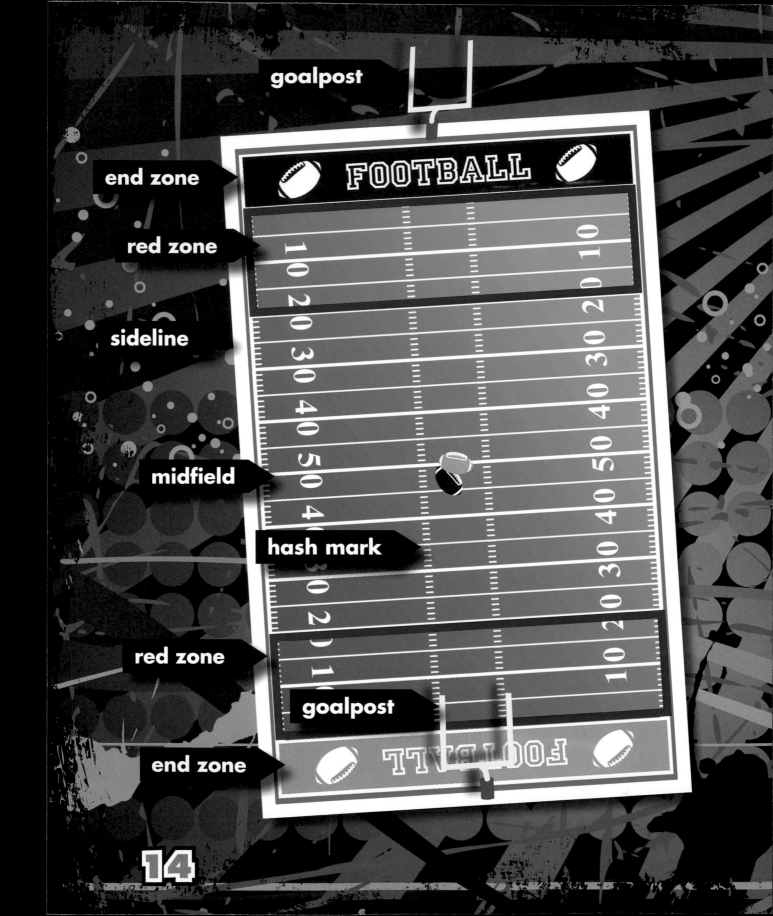

goalpost

end zone

red zone

sideline

midfield

hash mark

red zone

goalpost

end zone

FOOTBALL

The Football Field

An NFL field is 100 yards long. At each end is an **end zone** that is another 10 yards deep. Short white **hash marks** on the field mark off every yard. Longer lines mark every five yards. Numbers on the field help fans know where the players are. Goalposts stand at the back of each end zone. On some plays, a team can kick the football through the goalposts to earn points. During the game, each team stands along one sideline of the field. Oakland Coliseum is covered with real grass. Some indoor NFL stadiums have **artificial**, or fake, grass.

During a game, the two teams stand on the sidelines. They usually stand near midfield, waiting for their turns to play. Coaches walk on the sidelines, too, along with cheerleaders and photographers.

15

Big Days!

The Oakland Raiders have had many great moments in their long history. Here are three of the greatest:

1967: The Raiders won the AFL championship. That gave them a spot in the second Super Bowl! But they lost the Super Bowl to the Green Bay Packers, 33–14.

1977: Oakland won its first Super Bowl. The "Silver and Black" beat the Minnesota Vikings, 32-14.

1984: The Raiders brought a Super Bowl title to their new home in Los Angeles. They whomped the Washington Redskins, 38–9.

Super Raiders! A hard-hitting defense was the key to the Raiders' first Super Bowl victory over the Minnesota Vikings.

Tough Days!

The Raiders can't win all their games. Some games or seasons don't turn out well. The players keep trying to play their best, though! Here are some painful memories from Raiders' history.

1962: The Raiders won only one game . . . their worst season!

2003: The Raiders won the AFC title. But they lost the Super Bowl to the Tampa Bay Buccaneers, 48–21.

2006: The Raiders won only two games. They also lost their last nine in a row!

Andrew Walter (16) lost the ball on this play. It was one of many bad moments in the Raiders' 2006 season.

Heroes Then . . .

Raiders **quarterback** Daryle Lamonica loved throwing long passes. He led the team to its first Super Bowl. His **center** was Jim Otto, who wore No. 00. He was the best center in the AFL for 10 years. Ken Stabler took over at quarterback. He was a lefty known as "The Snake." **Linebacker** Ted Hendricks was big, tall, and strong. He was called "The Stork." Fred Biletnikoff didn't have a funny nickname. He just had sticky hands that caught dozens of touchdowns. In the 1980s, **running back** Marcus Allen helped the Raiders win a Super Bowl. He was a terrific runner. Tim Brown was a record-setting **receiver**.

1982–1992
MARCUS ALLEN
Running Back

Tim Brown (left) is the Raiders' all-time leader in catches and receiving yards.

23

Heroes Now . . .

Leading the Raiders today is big quarterback JaMarcus Russell. He's heavier and stronger than many players at his position. His key running back is Darren McFadden. Darren is quick and strong. He's great at finding holes in the defense to run through. **Tight end** Zach Miller catches lots of passes from Russell. Zach is big and strong and hard to tackle once he's caught the ball. On defense, the best player has the toughest name: Nnamdi Asomugha. He plays **cornerback** and stops the other team from catching passes.

JAMARCUS RUSSELL
Quarterback

DARREN MCFADDEN
Running Back

ZACH MILLER
Tight End

25

Gearing Up

Oakland Raiders players wear lots of gear to help keep them safe. They wear pads from head to toe. Check out this picture of Darren McFadden and learn what NFL players wear.

The Football

NFL footballs are made of four pieces of leather. White laces help the quarterback grip and throw the ball. Inside the football is a rubber bag that holds air.

Football Fact

NFL footballs don't have white lines around them. Only college teams use footballs with those lines.

shoulder pad

chest pad

helmet

thigh pad

knee pad

cleats

27

Sports Stats

Note: All numbers are through the 2008 season.

Touchdowns

TOUCHDOWN MAKERS

These players have scored the most touchdowns for the Raiders.

PLAYER	TOUCHDOWNS
Tim Brown	104
Marcus Allen	98

PASSING FANCY

Top Raiders quarterbacks

PLAYER	PASSING YARDS
Ken Stabler	19,078
Rich Gannon	17,585

Quarterbacks

RUN FOR GLORY

Top Raiders running backs

PLAYER	RUSHING YARDS
Marcus Allen	8,545
Mark van Eeghen	5,907

Running backs

Receivers

CATCH A STAR
Top Raiders receivers

PLAYER	CATCHES
Tim Brown	1,070
Fred Biletnikoff	589

TOP DEFENDERS
Raiders defensive records

Most **interceptions**: Lester Hayes, 39;
Willie Brown, 39
Most **sacks**: Greg Townsend, 107.5

Defenders

COACH
Most Coaching Wins

John Madden, 112

Coach

Glossary

artificial fake, not real

center a player on the offensive line who snaps, or hikes, the ball to the quarterback

cornerback a player who covers the other team's receivers and tries to keep them from making catches

defense players who are trying to keep the other team from scoring

end zone a 10-yard-deep area at each end of the field

hash marks short white lines that mark off each yard on the football field

interceptions catches made by defensive players

linebacker a defensive player who begins each play standing behind the main defensive line

line of scrimmage the place where the two teams face off when a play starts

logo a picture or symbol that stands for a sports team

offense players who have the ball and are trying to score

quarterback the key offensive player who starts each play and passes or hands off to a teammate

receiver an offensive player who catches forward passes

running back an offensive player who runs with the football and catches passes

sacks tackles of a quarterback behind the line of scrimmage

Super Bowl the NFL's annual championship game

tight end an offensive player who catches passes and blocks

touchdowns six-point scores made by carrying or catching the ball in the end zone

Find Out More

BOOKS

Buckley, James Jr. *The Scholastic Ultimate Book of Football.* New York: Scholastic, 2009.

Frisch, Aaron. *The History of the Oakland Raiders.* Mankato, MN: Creative Education, 2005.

Madden, John, and Bill Gutman. *Heroes of Football.* New York: Dutton, 2006.

Polzer, Tim. *Play Football! A Guide for Young Players from the National Football League.* New York: DK Publishing, 2002.

WEB SITE

Visit our Web site for lots of links about the Oakland Raiders and other NFL football teams:

childsworld.com/links

Note to Parents, Teachers, and Librarians: We routinely verify our Web links to make sure they are safe, active sites—so encourage your readers to check them out!

Index

About the Author

K. C. Kelley is a huge football fan! He has written dozens of books on football and other sports for young readers. K. C. used to work for NFL Publishing and has covered several Super Bowls.